Fountain
Network

*A missionary movement to release,
encourage and equip followers of Jesus.*

FOUNTAIN STUDY GUIDES

WALKING IN FREEDOM

Other titles from Freddy Hedley

Listening for Mission
(with Steve Croft and Bob Hopkins)

Lessons from Antioch

Coaching for Missional Leadership
(with Bob Hopkins)

A Pioneer's Understanding of the Church
(with Bob Hopkins)

The Lost Story: The Scroll of Remembrance

The God of Page One

The Eden Complex
(due for publication, Spring 2013)

WALKING IN FREEDOM

A journey through Galatians

Freddy Hedley

Rehoboth

Media

ISBN 978-0-9574813-0-5

Cover design by MPH.

Published by Rehoboth Media
The Well Christian Centre
Swaffham Road
Ashill
Norfolk
IP25 7BT

CONTENTS

FOREWORD

The Fountain Study series has been produced to help individuals and small groups of every kind dig deeper into God's word. It is rooted in the conviction that Bible study is primarily intended to be a journey of discovery assisted by the Holy Spirit as our tour guide. The purpose of this study guide is merely to set the direction and pace of that journey.

Each section contains a commentary which is intended to be a framework for understanding the context and content of the passage. This is followed by a focus on application with the author sharing some thoughts on how this may be applied to real life today. The questions are intended to stimulate not just discussion but a sharing of lives in a way that leads to action and transformation.

To accompany this book, there is also a downloadable resource available with each of these studies laid out in a printable A4 format for easier use in small groups. This costs £1 and can be purchased by emailing Rehoboth Media at admin@folchurch.co.uk

In this particular study, Freddy Hedley examines the theme of freedom in Paul's letter to the Galatian church. Paul's theology is complex. Freddy has a knack of presenting old truth in fresh, creative ways which stimulate thought and bring about change.

Whether you find yourself studying this book on your own, in the company of one or two others around a coffee table, leading a group in a more formal setting, or gathering a few friends and colleagues in the workplace, may this series deepen your relationship with the author of life and satisfy your thirst for the living God.

Stephen Mawditt

Introduction

THE PROMISE OF FREEDOM

When it comes to how we live, God has always been very clear. He wants us to be free. Indeed, he will move heaven and earth to make sure we can live in complete freedom. It is his top priority and has been from the very beginning.

Consider the following passages from God's Word:

> *I will walk about in freedom, for I have*
> *sought out your precepts.*
> **Psalm 119:45**

> *The Spirit of the Lord is on me ...*
> *He has sent me to proclaim freedom*
> *for the prisoners.*
> **Luke 4:18 (quoting Isaiah 61:1)**

> *Creation itself will be liberated from its*
> *bondage to decay and brought into the glorious*
> *freedom of the children of God.*
> **Romans 8:21**

Now the Lord is the Spirit, and where the Spirit of the Lord is, there is freedom.
2 Corinthians 3:17

In him [Jesus] and through faith in him we may approach God with freedom and confidence.
Ephesians 3:12

Speak and act as those who are going to be judged by the law that gives freedom.
James 2:12

Live as free men ...
1 Peter 2:16

When it comes to how we live, God has always been very clear. He wants us to be free. Indeed, he will move heaven and earth to make sure we can live in complete freedom. It is his top priority and has been from the very beginning.

When God placed Adam in the Garden of Eden his first words to him were, "You are free to eat from any tree in the garden." (Genesis 2:16) In the days of Moses, God set his people free from slavery in Egypt. In the days of Israel's exile in Babylon, he spoke through Isaiah to assure them that he would come to set the captives free (Isaiah 61:1). And then came Jesus to fulfil that promise.

If we were still in any doubt, Paul, Peter and James repeatedly told us of God's freedom in their letters, and in Galatians, Paul throws all subtlety aside:

It is for freedom that Christ has set us free.
Galatians 5:1

He is not only talking about freedom from sin, but from fear, inadequacy, habitual behaviour, doubt, sickness, destitution, and whatever else you can add to the list. There is no aspect of life that escapes God's promise of freedom, and nothing to match the feeling of being completely free. I am reminded of Paul saying to the Philippian church:

Brothers, I do not consider myself yet to have taken hold of it. But one thing I do: Forgetting what is behind and straining towards what is ahead, I press on towards the goal to win the prize for which God has called me heaven-wards in Christ Jesus.
Philippians 3:13-14

Freedom is my prize, and I want to press on towards the goal to claim it. It is the prize for a race that Jesus has already won, with my number pinned to his shirt. His is the victory, mine is the podium! And this, I believe, is something he wants us all to fix our eyes on.

He wants all of us to have a passionate desire for the "life to the full" that Jesus promises. He wants us all to walk in freedom. This is what we are called to do, what we were created to do, and when we walk in freedom we feel complete.

The difficulty lies in seeing what imprisons us. It can be easy to think we are free, or to assume we are free, simply because our chains are invisible to us. So we become accustomed to them, even accepting of them. Our expectations drop and we look to God for less, because we don't realise there is more to hope for.

This is a lie of the enemy, and one that it all too easy to believe, even to tell to ourselves. But it is not God's hope for us, and when we do find ourselves in this trap, it is so important to rest on the freedom we have already experienced. So often I have found in my own life that it wasn't until I experienced freedom that I could recognise captivity, and celebrating that freedom has a way of drawing my attention to where I cannot yet celebrate.

God so desperately wants to help us see more of what holds us down so we can reject it and step into the freedom that has already been won for us. Only then will we experience what true freedom is like, what being complete is like, just as God intends for us.

Of course, sometimes we are only too aware of what holds us captive. Let me tell you a story. Try not to laugh. Not too much, anyway. When I was ten years old I got myself locked in a disused public ladies lavatory! Now obviously as a rule I would be reluctant to tell this story, as it is probably the most embarrassing moment in my life, except that it is also the moment in my life when I felt the most imprisoned.

Let me elaborate. When I was young, some friends and I would regularly play together in the local park that backed onto my back garden. We would have all sorts of adventures, build camps and generally run about. But if we were feeling especially brave we would creep into the garden of the disused park warden's house.

This garden was surrounded by tall dark hedges and because it was disused it was heavily overgrown. It was attached to what used to be the park warden's house, which had long been abandoned. The windows were boarded up and it was in all ways lifeless. This gave it an aura of mystery and danger, so it would have been unnatural for four over adventurous boys not to go exploring.

To begin with this was filled with risk and excitement, and each time we went back we would go a little further in. However, after a while we were so used to this adventure that we would think nothing of going in openly without a second thought. The garden had become a comfortable place, and we began to look for the next boundary.

The next building along from the deserted warden's house was the old disused public lavatory. It had been locked up as long as I had ever known, was covered with graffiti, and it seemed to be an even more scary place than the deserted house. It was the perfect next adventure.

To begin with, we did not mean to go in. After all, it was locked, and we were not into breaking and entering! We intended to build adventures around it, try and look in the windows, that kind of thing. But then we discovered that the ladies toilet's lock was broken and we could get in. The temptation was too great and so cautiously we entered.

I don't know what mysteries we were expecting, because it was just a normal loo, but we felt so dangerous, walking in forbidden places. Not only were we somewhere no-one was allowed, we were four boys in a girls toilet! For a couple of minutes we explored with relish, but then one of my friends accidentally knocked against the entrance door, it slammed shut and we fell into darkness.

We tried to open the door, but it had locked itself. We were trapped. To begin with I found this quite funny. But then a few moments went by and the reality of our situation gradually sank in. I began to panic, as did my friends. We banged against the door and walls in a frenzy, shouting for help, and we cried and started blaming one another. We could see the park through the keyhole, but it must have been a quiet day, because nobody walked past for ages. I felt so utterly helpless and I couldn't see an end to it. All I could think was that we would never be found.

On reflection this was a bit melodramatic and of course, eventually, someone did walk past and they were easily able to fetch my parents and the park warden and we were let out. In reality, we can't have been there for more than half an hour. However, at the time it felt much worse than it was and I was left with three lasting impressions, which endure to this day.

The first was the extreme embarrassment that set in within a few minutes of being rescued. The second was the sense of overwhelming fear and helplessness whilst we were trapped. But most importantly, the third was the feeling of complete joy at being released. The sun shone brighter, the sky was bluer, the air was fresher. I had tasted freedom and I felt like the world had been renewed.

This may be a trivial example of captivity, but this is also something that we all are subject to in our lives. Each one of us has areas of our lives where we are trapped. These captivities express themselves in all sorts of different ways – addiction, compulsive behaviour, culture, habit, oppression, temptation, upbringing, illness, peer-pressure, stress, low self-esteem, shyness, debt, crime, and so on and so on.

For some of us it may be small things, or hidden things that we can often ignore, or at least not draw attention to. For others it can be things that dominate every aspect of life. Whatever it is, big or small, we all know what it means to be trapped.

Jesus recognised this. His whole purpose in life was to address this, even to the extent of releasing humanity from its captivity away from heaven caused by failure to follow the Jewish Law. When Jesus returned home after forty days in the desert he went to his local synagogue and read this messianic prophecy from Isaiah:

He has sent me to bind up the broken hearted,
to proclaim freedom for the captives and release
from darkness for the prisoners.
Isaiah 61:1

He told the rapt listeners that this passage had been fulfilled in their hearing (Luke 4:21), essentially claiming this to be his role in life as the Son of God. Jesus was in the business of bringing freedom. He felt the pain and helplessness of those that were trapped, and he lived to see people released into the joy of being free. The whole gospel rests on this.

Paul knew this. He himself had been held captive by his pharisaic upbringing. This had prompted him to the hatred and persecution of followers of Jesus and to be confined by a law he couldn't live up to.

It led him to become, at the very least, a condoner and organiser of murder and persecution, and probably a protagonist:

something that must have been so contrary to how he would have seen himself as a young man, zealous to live for God.

But then he was set free by Jesus in dramatic circumstances and the impact was so powerful that he gave all his energy for the rest of his life to spread this message of freedom as far as he could. And in the process he helped to start many new faith communities.

In his first missionary journey from Antioch, made with Barnabas, Paul (then called Saul) travelled through several towns in the region of Galatia. Pisidian Antioch, Iconium, Lystra and Derbe (Acts 13-14) all made up this region of Asia Minor, and the book of Acts records many church communities that were started there.

These churches are formed from a mixture of Jews and Gentiles, which to begin with seemed to work remarkably well. However, at some point between Paul and Barnabas returning to Antioch (Acts 14) and their leaving for the Council of Jerusalem (Acts 15), it seems that news of these churches reached them that suggested the Jewish Christians had fallen back into their Jewish traditions and Law, and the freedom that Paul had preached was under threat of being lost.

So, in around AD49 he wrote the first of his letters (that we have record of at least) to these churches to reaffirm the reality and vitality of the freedom that Christ had brought. This is the letter to the Galatians in the New Testament. Right from the opening greeting Paul made his intentions for this letter clear, wishing them grace from Christ, "who gave himself for our sins to *rescue us* from the present evil age" (Galatians 1:4, italics mine).

This letter was, and is, about freedom. As Paul tackled the particular issues that the Galatian churches were struggling with, he identified six ways that God had set them free, and to reinforce them he tackled each of them twice. He structured the letter to focus first on the foundations of the Galatians' lives, from their identity to their most precious beliefs, before shifting his attention to how these freedoms should shape the way they lived.

In this short book we are going to explore what God, through Paul, has to say about freedom in six studies. What have we been set free from? What does our freedom look like? How do we live in freedom?

To do this, rather than taking the book a chapter at a time, we are going to take each freedom in turn. Therefore, each study will include two passages, one from the first half of the letter, one from the second half.

Each study begins with a short exposition commentary on the passage, followed by an application commentary, and concludes with some questions to work through, to help you explore how these issues impact to your life today, and how can you walk in the freedom that Christ has won for you.

If you are using this book for small group studies, feel completely free to use each of these sections as you feel best. You may want to give the commentaries to those leading each study to inform their preparation or you may want to read them out as part of the study itself, however works best for you. And please do add your own questions as they occur, either in preparation or during your study together.

However you use this book, I pray it is helpful, encouraging and spurs you on to walk ever more in the freedom God has given you.

WALKING IN FREEDOM

Six Studies in Galatians

Study One

FREE TO KNOW THE GOSPEL

Galatians 1:1-10 and 3:26-4:7

I am astonished that you are so quickly deserting the one who called you by the grace of Christ and are turning to a different gospel – which is really no gospel at all.

Galatians 1:6

COMMENTARY

It would seem that not long after Paul travelled through Galatia with Barnabas, another message in conflict with the gospel Paul had preached had begun to take hold. Paul had spoken of a Jesus who loved both Jew and Gentile – who wanted to be in relationship with all of his creation, and not just a "chosen" portion of it.

However, a group known as Judaisers disagreed and said that Jesus was the Jewish Messiah, and so for Jews only. Gentiles could still be saved, but only if they converted to Judaism. Therefore, they must be circumcised and recognise that their salvation was dependent upon observance of the Law.

When news of this reached Paul, he quickly dispatched a letter reminding them of the gospel they had first responded to. That gospel (good news) was that God had broken all the barriers. He had broken the barriers between man and God; between Jew and Gentile; between slave and free; between man and woman; between law and grace; between sin and salvation; between death and life.

The good news was that everyone was invited into an intimate relationship with the Father, through the Son by the power of the Holy Spirit. The good news was that everyone was invited to live in unity for eternity in the Kingdom of God, starting immediately, and to experience and exercise the love and power of the Kingdom. This was the gospel that the Galatian churches had first embraced. This was the message that opened their hearts for Jesus to enter in, but they had forgotten it.

The problem is that when things get tough it is a human instinct to revert to familiar territory. The Bible is full of this happening. When the Hebrews found the desert tough they cried out to return to Egypt (Exodus 16:3, 17:3). When the tribes of Reuben, Gad and Manasseh were faced with the unknown prospects of the Promised Land their faith failed and they requested land on the desert side of the Jordan (Numbers 32). When the rich young ruler was challenged about giving up his fortune, he retreated to his riches (Matthew 19:16-22).

Living according to the gospel is not easy. It may involve eternal freedom, joy, grace, experience of God, true revelation of identity, but it also involves sacrifice, persecution and taking risks as we walk in faith.

When the Galatians began to move beyond the first joys of faith, and they experienced some of the challenges, it was instinctive for them to be open to the temptations of the familiar. For most of them that was Jewish culture. For them, the Jewish Law may have guaranteed a life governed by rules, most of which were impossible to keep to, but it was constant. It had always been there to assure them of when they were "in the right."

And, when they were not, the Law was there to show them how to make amends. It meant a personal relationship with impossible, but at least they knew where they stood.

Life must have seemed far less certain, more dangerous even, in a gospel without the Law. So, when the Judaisers came with the message: "Don't worry, God hasn't taken the Law away," they must have been easy words to accept. And so they did, to the point of denying the gospel they had first responded to, and preaching a gospel of sin and judgement according to an unobtainable Law. In other words an anti-gospel … bad news!

However, Paul knew that faith which is easy really is no faith at all. His response is quick and stern. The gospel may be challenging, but then so is freedom. It comes with hard choices and risks, but it leads to a life beyond the most wondrous dreams. Paul began his letter with this message, which he revisited in the middle: the gospel has not changed. It is still for all, and it is still for freedom.

APPLICATION

How often do you consider how you first found Jesus? Jesus was at work in your life before you knew anything about it. He was shaping the circumstances and calling your name even before you were born.

When you found him, he had long before found you. And when you found him it was because he had reached into your life at that time (or over a process of time) when your heart was in a place to hear and accept him.

And when your heart did hear, and when it responded, it was because a particular aspect of the gospel had reached in and touched you. It may have been a conviction of your sin, with the promise of forgiveness; or it may have been an experience of God the powerful intervener; or it may have been a word of knowledge showing a God who knows you fully and loves you completely; or any number of other things.

What first caused you to say yes to Jesus? How was Jesus first consciously good news for you? In other words, what is the Gospel for you?

I do not mean that for some forgiveness of sin may not be the gospel. That is certainly true for everyone. But that may not have been the good news we first responded to. For me, it was a realisation that God had a purpose for me to fulfil and that if I didn't fulfil it, no-one else could. This led me to realise that I wasn't good enough to fit this purpose, and so I came to the cross of the only one who is good enough.

Whatever the gospel you first responded to, hear these words spoken by Paul to the Galatians: "If anybody is preaching to you a gospel other than what you accepted, let him be eternally condemned!" (Galatians 1:9). As Christians, we must stand in confidence on the good news that first called us to God, because God wants us to be free from the bad news that fills the world.

We need to grasp onto the good news in order that our faith may be built up and we might be strengthened to step into the hardships that can accompany our commitment to follow Jesus.

As you look back over your life since becoming a Christian, are there areas of your faith where you have become disappointed? Or have doubts crept in where you have waited for a God who has never arrived, at least not for a long time? Or have some of the difficulties and realities of life caused your faith to become less of a priority in your mind each day?

These are some of the ways that we can forget the Gospel that we first responded to. And if we do, our tendency will be to return to what is comfortable and familiar, whether that is less commitment to prayer, reading the bible or church; or whether it leads us back into areas of sin, or unhelpful and unhealthy life choices. Are there areas of your life where you are returning to what you find familiar and comfortable, instead of living according to the promise of the gospel you first responded to?

Paul encouraged us to remember the gospel we are committed to and not to let other people, circumstances or hardship get in the way of reaching for the promise of "life to the full" with God. In contrast to the temptations of the Galatians, we need to hold firm to our faith in the gospel and invite Jesus into every area of our life. This way it will be our walk with Jesus that becomes familiar, so that when things get tough, we will turn to him first. This takes time and commitment, but the fruit is that we will be completely free to know the gospel in every area of our life.

Walking in Freedom

STUDY QUESTIONS

How did you first become a Christian?

If you are studying in a group, share this with someone else.

Notes:

What was it about the gospel that you first responded to?

Notes:

Do you still live with the same commitment to this aspect of the gospel as you did then?

Notes:

If so, what are the opportunities for your Christian life to continue to grow in this area of the gospel?

Notes:

If not, what do you feel has drawn you away from Jesus as you first knew him?

Notes:

What one thing could you commit to doing to live more in the freedom of the gospel?

Notes:

Study Two

FREE FROM FORMER SELF

Galatians 1:11-24 and 4:8-20

They only heard the report: "The man who formerly persecuted us is now preaching the faith he once tried to destroy." And they praised God because of me.

Galatians 1:13-17, 22-24

COMMENTARY

Paul knew more than most that mud sticks. Before he first encountered Jesus on the road to Damascus, Paul (then known as Saul) was a Pharisaic Jew. As such, his whole life was rooted in the Law and any threat to the authority of the Holy Scriptures, particularly the Law, was an offence of the highest order to him. He was well known to be fiercely committed to the cause of opposing blasphemy.

When the followers of Jesus became more and more of a public movement that clearly would not go away quietly, Saul was right at the heart of organising the persecution that forced so much of the church to scatter (read Acts 8:1-3). Clearly he had held a significant level of authority to be able to do this. He had also been present (though apparently not actively involved) at the stoning and murder of Stephen, and who knows what other violence he condoned in order to "destroy the church," as Acts 8 describes it.

Consequently, and probably inevitably, his remarkable conversion after seeing a vision of the risen Jesus was treated with a great deal of suspicion by the early church. God intervened directly with Ananias to ensure Saul had a contact who would know of his genuine conversion, but it would take the discernment of someone as central and trusted as Barnabas to convince the apostles of his authenticity. Even then it would take some time, and a lot of personal sacrifice for the cause of spreading the gospel, before he was accepted by all into the church.

This struggle was largely behind Paul by the time of his contact with the Galatians, but it continued to mark his everyday life. For him the aspect of the gospel that he had responded to was that his former life did not need to dictate his future life. He had caused more harm to the church than most, and yet Jesus had forgiven him and chosen him to lead the way in extending the church to the Gentiles across Asia Minor and Europe.

He had been transformed by God's grace, and been given freedom from his former self. No longer was Paul the enemy of Jesus. No longer was he the enemy of the church. No longer was he bound by the restrictions and unobtainable salvation of the Law. Now he was forgiven - old life forgotten. Now he was a champion of the faith.

Paul's testimony shows how God can even turn our former self into an advantage, no matter how bad it may have been. As people saw Paul and heard him preach they knew that this was the same man who had persecuted the church; the same man who had been so condemning of the same faith he now proclaimed.

This gave his message authority as he was preaching the transformation that Jesus brings and they could see it right before their very eyes. In chapter 1, verse 24 Paul says, "And they praised God because of me." His life became a testimony of the transforming power of Jesus.

Paul had been set free from his former self, to the point where it has become a badge of honour - evidence of God's goodness. But when he hears about the Galatian churches returning to Jewish ways he points to the danger of embracing the former self once again (chapter 4:8-20). It is the route back into slavery, back into human weakness holding them away from God, and he pleads with them to recognise what they are doing.

Choosing "the easy path" is exactly that - easy - but it holds us in captivity and withholds the power of the Kingdom in and through our lives, so that we cannot grow and cannot live in the joy that Paul says they are now missing (chapter 4, verse 15).

APPLICATION

Does your past come back to haunt you? Do you find yourself doubting your worthiness of living in God's presence because of things you have done, said and thought before you became a Christian? Do you even find yourself falling back into old behaviours and mindsets?

We are all created to be champions of the faith, but one of the things that can hold us back from embracing the life God has for us is a nagging sense that we just don't warrant the confidence He has placed in us. We are not strong enough or wise enough. But more importantly, we are not good enough.

We have done, and continue to do, too many things in our life that are not good. Our discipline is poor, our faith too small, our past too littered with sins or bad and painful experiences for us ever to recover enough to serve Jesus effectively. We can't do it.

Jesus promises freedom from these fears that hold us back. More than that, he can even turn our weaknesses and the demons in our past into strengths for the Kingdom.

How?

Freedom comes from first acknowledging that the enemy's lies are cloaked in truth. We do not meet the mark. But the cross means we do not have to, and this is what the enemy conveniently forgets to mention! We need only to step out in the knowledge that Jesus does meet the mark, and meets it on our behalf. Realising this helps us take steps of faith and reminds us of the grace that not only saved us from death, but works through us to save others.

Freedom also comes from remembering that where we are weak God is strong. Sometimes it can feel like God asks the impossible of us. It certainly must have felt like that for Paul as he reflected on God's call for him (of all people) to be the face of Jesus across Asia Minor and Europe. The rich young ruler was asked to give away his money, and that was a step too far for him. He resorted to what was familiar (see the last study) and his walk with Jesus stopped as he walked away with his riches. But Jesus' response was to say "What is impossible for man is possible for God."

God can make the impossible possible. So we can follow God into impossible places and He makes them possible. In the same way, He turns the impossible nature of our weaknesses into advantages.

It is the same for our past, what Paul elsewhere refers to as our former self. Our future is not dependent on our past, but on Jesus alone. Otherwise there would be no way Paul could have become the leader he became. We do not need to feel guilty about our past, because Jesus died so that it doesn't even need to be an issue.

We do not need to be bound by the wounds that our past has given us, because Jesus offers healing as we follow him. We do not need to be limited by our experiences of the past, because Jesus promises life to the full, with new opportunities and new gifts. We do not need to turn opportunities down because in the past we would not have been confident enough, because Jesus gives us the authority we need to go wherever he asks us to (Paul was given the authority of an apostle).

As we see though the life of Paul, our weaknesses and our life before we knew Jesus can even be a powerful testimony to non-Christians. If we are open about our struggles, and if we testify to how Jesus has transformed us, then people will see the difference that Jesus makes and will praise God because of us.

But we do not need to be bound by our former self. Through Christ's death we are given freedom from our former self, just as Paul was free, and we too can be champions of the faith and see others praise God because of Jesus at work in our lives.

STUDY QUESTIONS

Can you recognise any areas of your life where you feel as though you cannot move forward with Jesus because of your past?

Notes:

Do you believe that Jesus can bring transformation and healing in the places where you have been weak or hurt in the past?

Notes:

What ways can you identify that Jesus has brought transformation in your life?

Notes:

Are you open about how you became a Christian with others around you, both Christian and non-Christian?

Notes:

What encouragements and challenges do you take from this passage in Galatians?

Notes:

What one thing can you do to increase your knowledge of your freedom from your "former self"?

Notes:

Study Three

FREE TO HEAR GOD'S CALLING

Galatians 2:1-10 and 4:21-31

Fourteen years later I went up again to Jerusalem ... They saw that I had been entrusted with the task of preaching the gospel to the Gentiles, just as Peter had been to the Jews.

Galatians 2:1, 7

COMMENTARY

God has a unique purpose for each of us. In fact we each have two purposes to fulfil in our lives. The first (that is shared by all of us) is to live in relationship with God, extending to eternal life in heaven. The second is the unique role God has given each of us in His created world. Let's begin by considering the second calling, since Paul addresses this first in 2:1-10. For Paul, his calling was to be an apostolic missionary, spreading the good news of Jesus amongst the Gentiles. This was not the kind of calling that many in the early church would ever have dreamed could even exist.

Surely, they would have thought, God had made it abundantly clear that He was the God of the Jews. It only followed that the salvation of Jesus must be for them, and not the very people that the Jewish Law had separated them from – people they had been raised to think of as "unclean." It must have been tempting for Paul to think the same. In fact, as a Pharisaic Jew, he must have held these views close to his heart his whole life. And so it is all the more extraordinary that someone who had grown up looking down on Gentiles was willing to spend the rest of his life living alongside them, loving them and offering them the hope of heaven.

However, as we have already explored, Paul was free from his former self. He was no longer bound by the constraints or expectations from his past. He was free to serve Jesus and fulfil the purpose for which he was created, so when he is called upon to preach the gospel to the Gentiles he is free to say yes.

Now let's consider the first calling, given to us all, which Paul comes to when he revisits this issue in 4:21-31. In fact, "calling" is not how Paul describes it - this puts the onus on us. Paul puts the onus on Jesus, who has taken the initiative over this purposeful area of our lives, describing it instead in terms of "the promise."

He then goes on to explain this concept with what would have been very familiar theological practise - exploring the lines of Abraham's two sons - but he applies it in a new way, showing how Isaac is the line of the promise, and all who respond to Jesus are a part of that line. So, having already offered the Galatians hope in their freedom from their "former self", he now offers them purpose for their identity in Christ - their new self.

We share the same two purposes today: to

respond to the promise and respond to the calling, and because of the life and love of Jesus we are free to say yes to both. The only issue is to discern what our personal calling is, which is easier said than done! Even Paul found this hard. In verse two he indicates that he was still unsure he had heard God correctly, and was nervous of being exposed as "running the race in vain." He was unsure enough to talk with the church leaders privately so he wouldn't look stupid, and yet he had every reason to be confident in his calling.

He describes going to Jerusalem "in response to a revelation" (2:2), suggesting that he had heard his call affirmed directly from God. He also had the fruit of what God had done in others to give him confidence, bringing with him the Greek Titus who had responded so strongly to Jesus without any inclination to become Judaised.

Also, when you look back at how Paul was converted (Acts 9:1-19), it is clear that Jesus speaks to Ananias about Paul's purpose, and it seems hard to believe that this wouldn't have been spoken about while Ananias sheltered Paul in Damascus.

And yet despite all of this Paul was anxious about declaring his calling to the Jerusalem church, and so he relied heavily on the discernment of the apostles. Thankfully, they agreed with him and sent both him and Barnabas back to Antioch with a recognised purpose to preach Jesus to the Gentiles, as they reaffirmed their own call to do the same amongst the Jews.

APPLICATION

So what might this discernment process have looked like? This section of Galatians raises the importance of knowing we are free to fulfil our purpose, and it does have some of the answers as to how to discern this purpose, but to really get to grips with this we need to look a little further afield at Paul's life to see some of how his discernment process worked.

This will not be an exhaustive list of how to discover God's call on your life, but here are a few suggestions for starters:

What is on your heart? What would you give anything to see happen in the church or the world? It may relate to particular people, as it did for Paul, or a particular ministry, or to a particular lifestyle. It could be to see social justice (the poor, homeless, political corruption, etc) or ecological responsibility. It could be a passion to use your money for God, or to express Jesus through action and work in the community. The Bible says that God will give us the desires of our heart (Psalm 37:4), so this is a very good place to start in assessing our call.

Is it consistent with God's truth? This means it will be founded on love; for his glory, not ours; an expression of the Gospel, etc. In particular, we should consider the gospel we first responded to. Each of us has responded to God's truth in a way that is particularly relevant to us, and this aspect of God's truth that has most impacted us is the aspect that we will be able to communicate with the most authority. The freedom God brings is most dramatically demonstrated by the freedom we have gained.

Has there been prophetic insight? This could be through words given by others, dreams, visions, inspired Scripture or circumstances. God is always speaking if only we will take the time to listen for his voice. He is always on the move if we will only watch for where he is leading. As you pray, be asking God to reveal his purpose for you through the prophetic ... and then expect him to answer.

What are your gifts? God promises to equip us for the work he calls us to, with knowledge, skills, talents and spiritual gifts. The gifts in particular are highlighted several times (1 Corinthians 12:1-11, Romans 12:6-8, Ephesians 4:1-13, 1 Peter 5:10-11), though probably never as a definitive list. Discerning the ways God has gifted us can be a huge help with discovering what he wants us to do.

Do others agree? It is almost universally true that others see more in us than we see in ourselves. This is true both of our strengths and our shortcomings. We have just mentioned how it can be helpful to test our gifts with others, and we can do the same with our calling. Pray with people you feel comfortable being accountable with. Share with them your passions and ideas, and ask them, "What do you think?"

Where has God put you? It may be that for some of us our passions and vision lead us to feel that we are called into serving Him away from where we live. For most of us, though, God has already placed us where He wants to work through us. You might understand this in terms of the town you live in, or the people you spend time with, or even your current life circumstances. Wherever it is that you recognise God has already brought you to, could it be that this is an indication of where God wants you to remain, following and serving him there?

STUDY QUESTIONS

There is just one question, but many ways to explore the answer. The question is this: **What is God's calling in your life right now?**

Try using the questions that are explored in the 'Response' section of this study to help you dig into this.

What is on your heart?

Notes:

Is it consistent with God's truth?

Notes:

Has there been prophetic insight?

Notes:

What are your gifts?

Notes:

Do others agree?

Notes:

Where has God put you?

Notes:

Study Four

FREE TO LIVE BY FAITH

Galatians 2:11-21 and 5:1-15

The life I live in the body, I live by faith in the Son of God, who loved me and gave himself for me. I do not set aside the grace of God, for if righteousness could be gained through the law, Christ died for nothing.

Galatians 2:20-21

COMMENTARY

The biggest issue that the New Testament church wrestled with in the years following Christ's resurrection was the tension between the life of freedom that Jesus offered, and the expectations of the Jewish faith, which had given birth to Christianity. In particular, tensions ran high concerning the importance or otherwise of the Jewish Law.

Outside of the church, the Jewish Pharisees and Sadducees were very clear on the matter: Christians were blasphemers and deniers of God's Holy Law. They felt so threatened by the uncontainable growth of this new movement that it led to segregation and persecution, to the point of having followers of Jesus killed.

After all, the Law was the guide and constant determining factor in the Jewish faith. It was the immovable object that maintained God's position in people's lives. It covered everything from worship and ritual, to washing and eating. There was not a single aspect of life omitted.

For the Jewish man who followed the Law to the letter their place in heaven was assured.

Indeed, faithful Jewish believers knew no other way to find God.

There was only one problem: it was completely impossible to follow. Humanity was simply too broken to comply. Despite the Law containing a complicated system of sacrifices and cleansing rituals to compensate for when people fell short, still their hearts strayed away from God. They were stuck in a rut: salvation was dependent on effort, but no amount of effort was ever enough.

Then came Jesus, and revealed the Law for what it always was: a revelation of God's holiness and an invitation to have a relationship with him - not a set of impossible rules to hold us at bay. He redefined this holiness in the contemporary world and then made the only sacrifice necessary to compensate for our failure to comply.

No longer were people bound to a life spent constantly fleeing death. Now they could have life to the full, pursuing a life that never ends, into the promise of an eternal relationship with the Father. Death, sin, uncleanness, it was all dealt with on the cross - by this one act of irrevocable grace. And why? "It was for freedom that Christ as set us free." (Galatians 5:1)

This was the gospel, the good news, that Paul had taken to the churches in Galatia, and initially they had welcomed it with open arms. But then, as we have already explored, the 'easier' message of the Judaisers came, promising Christian salvation exercised through the familiar shelter of the Law, and no issue exhibited this tension more than attitudes towards circumcision.

When Paul heard that the Galatian churches were struggling more than most with these issues, he saw it immediately for what it was – a return to life without grace. A return to life spent fleeing death, unable to embrace life to the full. And so, having started his letter by reminding them of the gospel they first responded to, Paul goes on to reassert their freedom from the Law,.

Jesus did not die so that they could continue in their old ways, striving as if they didn't need the cross in the first place. Jesus died so that they might be completely free from everything that held them away from God's throne, so that they could live by faith: "faith expressing itself through love" (5:6). To God it was more important that his people could live in relationship with him than they worked themselves into the ground trying to become holy enough to not feel ashamed in his presence.

This unmanageable burden had been removed, at great personal cost, by a heavenly Father who loved them too much not to go to any length to restore them to his side.

APPLICATION

We are offered the same amazing grace today as Paul described nearly two thousand years ago. And yet despite this, it is still so easy to fall back into striving for our own salvation.

We want to please God, but the only way we are taught to please people is by doing good things for them – earning their pleasure, earning their respect, earning their trust. We get caught up in trying to please God the same way we would try and please Auntie Mildred.

We show our love for people, and try to please them, in ways they can see. Acts of kindness, going out of our way, making time, buying gifts, and so forth. But God sees more than people do. He can see inside our hearts.

He knows how we feel, what our motives are, how much we have changed, what hurts us, what brings us joy. He sees when we use the gifts He gave us, he sees when we make great personal sacrifices, he sees when we forgive others.

These are the choices that please God. It's not that He doesn't want us to do good things, but we do them because we love God and the people around us, not because we can get something personally out of it.

God wants us to have an honest relationship with Him, where we allow Him to transform us from within, and we are willing to let him transform others through us, through our prayers, our words and the integrity of our lives. This is what really matters to God, and Jesus' death and resurrection means that we are free to move forwards with God in these ways, and give up to Him the burden of working for our place in heaven.

This was the gospel that Paul had shared in Galatia, and this is the gospel that we receive when we recognise Jesus as the saviour and leader of our life today.

Just as Paul was reaffirming to the Galatians that they really were free from the Law – free to receive this outrageous grace – so we are free to do the same. We do not need to fall back on our old ways, or to strive to earn our place in heaven. We cannot do it.

Nor can we earn God's love, or his respect, nor allay our shame even just a little so we can at least claim some of the credit for our salvation. It is all beyond us. But this great prize of eternal life is still firmly within our grasp because Jesus hands it to us freely, for no greater exchange than the acknowledgement that it is Jesus who offers it.

We are free from the burden of striving to be good Christians. We do not need to run ourselves into the ground as we look only to the ways we can avoid hell. Jesus' grace means that we can leave these worries behind and move forwards in our faith in the certainty that death cannot catch us up, no matter how often we stumble.

It is to his grace we hold. Jesus wants to take us to the point where he is so familiar to us that even when we are pressed to the point of breaking, all we can do is turn to him, and receive his freedom.

STUDY QUESTIONS

What are the 'rules' that we have created for our Christian lives today?

Notes:

Do you find these Christian 'rules' helpful to having a dynamic walk with Jesus, or a hindrance?

Notes:

Can you spot areas in your life where you are striving for spiritual success?

Notes:

How do you think you can submit more to God's grace, and allow Him to take responsibility for your righteousness?

Notes:

What might a life free from the burdens of working for salvation look like for you?

Notes:

Study Five

FREE TO RECEIVE THE SPIRIT

Galatians 3:1-14 and 5:16-26

Clearly no-one is justified before God by the law, because "The righteous will live by faith" ... so that by faith we might receive the promise of the Spirit.

Galatians 3:11, 14

COMMENTARY

By this point in the letter a process has clearly emerged: the process of faith growing to maturity. It begins with a revelation that God has set us free **from** something (studies 1 & 2), grows into a revelation that God has set us free **for** something (studies 3 & 4), and now we find that it flourishes with a revelation that God has set us free **with** something.

All of the freedom Paul has described so far only begins to look like faith (which literally means belief in action), when we embrace our freedom to receive the Holy Spirit. And as we go back into the book of Acts and read the accounts of how the Galatian churches were started, we can see that this was right at the heart of their formation.

Barnabas and Paul preached the good news, and many responded. But it was as these new believers continued to follow Jesus after Barnabas and Paul had left that the Holy Spirit came upon them in power and sealed their hope (read Acts 13:48-52 for a clear example of this in the Galatian town of Pisidian Antioch).

However, despite their experience of receiving the Holy Spirit in their first days of faith, and despite their remaining true to Christ and continuing to grow in both faith and numbers through many early difficulties (Acts 14:21-22), still they were open to false prophets coming among them and convincing them of a cheapened grace.

Paul was dismayed, but he knew that the key to a life in tune with God was living in the power of the Holy Spirit. As with all six freedoms raised in this letter, he discussed the Holy Spirit twice.

In 3:1-14 he assuring them that faith is not about striving and effort, but about allowing the Spirit to work within them to bring their salvation (v4) and through them to bring kingdom transformation (v5). He relates receiving the Spirit to the freedom from Law he is in the middle of affirming, reminding them that Abraham lived before the Law and yet was held as the highest model of faith.

His freedom was assured because of his relationship with God - a relationship, Paul says, we can now have again because of the cross. Only now that relationship is so much more intimate and powerful because the Holy Spirit dwells within us.

The Galatian churches seem to have forgotten all of this. It seems almost unthinkable to Paul that anyone could rely on their own strength rather than trust in the Holy Spirit, but that is what they have done. They have fallen back on the Law to guide their life and bring them salvation.

Paul calls them, "You foolish Galatians!" (v1) and considers them bewitched, as he reminds them that it wasn't the law that brought them freedom, but the Holy Spirit. It wasn't the law that revealed Christ to them, but the grace of God. It wasn't the law that would redeem them, but Jesus.

Then, in 5:16-26 he turns to what life ought to look like with the Spirit, describing first the specific areas of life - which had presumably been rife in Galatia at the time - that would be swept aside as the Holy Spirit overpowered the sinful nature, and second, the fruit of the Spirit which will replace the former weeds of the former self.

Fruit is the way that plants and trees pass on the best of themselves, and as we know from Jesus' teaching about the vine (John 15), the idea isn't to be at your most fruitful immediately, but to become more fruitful as you go through seasons of growth, interspersed with times of pruning back to the vine. Paul would certainly have known this teaching very well.

So the picture isn't necessarily so much one of sinless perfection, which can leave us assuming that we can't have the Spirit within us, because our lives are not yet free of weeds and full of fruit. It may be that Paul is encouraging us to be eager to pass on the best of ourselves (keeping "in step with the Spirit" as he puts it in v25) in the hope of seeing the fruits of the Spirit grow more in our lives as we pass them on.

APPLICATION

God's greatest hope for us is that we will become his dwelling place, so that we might know him intimately and he might influence the world because of us. When we receive the Holy Spirit we carry God through our every experience and feeling.

He shares our joys, our triumphs, our pains and our failures. He understands how we feel and He is able to comfort us, encourage us, guide and direct us, convict us, refresh us, transform us and work through us.

When God first created Adam and Eve, he lived alongside them so intimately in Eden that nothing was hidden. It was only when they ate the fruit that they chose to hide themselves, and the consequences were catastrophic.

It took God generations and the sacrifice of his only son to bring us back to a place where we can walk so openly with Him again. God has reclaimed our relationship with Him through His grace, he offers it anew to us each day, and there is no higher calling on our life than to accept.

And it is a daily acceptance. It is so easy to fall back on our own strength or to a way of life where God is pushed to the edges, so that our relationship with him becomes less meaningful. But God gives us the opportunity to turn back to him every day - Jesus calls this repentance (literally, to change your mind) - and in response he renews our freedom to receive the Holy Spirit.

The question is, how do we receive this amazing gift? Paul seems to address this in 3:1-14, and we might identify three steps:

Step one: recognise God's voice

Paul says that the Holy Spirit is given because *we believe what we have heard* (v2 and 5). Throughout Acts we read examples of people recognising that God was speaking through Paul and Barnabas.

There are many voices calling us in many directions in our life, be they from ourselves, society, the media, etc (and through all of these, the devil) - but there is also God's voice inviting us to follow Him. And when we hear His voice there is a difference. It burns within our hearts (Acts 24:32) and demands our attention.

We might call that conviction or a sense of his presence. Then we have a choice. Do we ignore him or do we turn our heads? Paul says that to receive the Holy Spirit we must turn. We must believe it was God's voice, and turn away from where we were heading and head instead towards him.

Step Two: Respond to God's voice

Paul describes this as "living by faith" (v11). In Romans 4:12, when discussing the same issue with the church in Rome, and using the same example of Abraham as a man who lived by faith, he describes this as "walking by faith."

Once we have heard God's voice we must begin to live and walk by faith. It is a choice. Faith is not passive – genuine faith is not dependant on "good works," and yet it cannot exist without them naturally flowing out.

The same is true today. We need to respond to God's voice by taking steps of faith, one at a time, until we find that we are walking by faith. The trouble is, as we all know, this is extremely hard. However, we have a God who understands how we struggle. Jesus has experienced all our struggles, and he has overcome. This is why we so desperately need the Holy Spirit – so that we are filled with the Spirit of the one who can overcome our struggles.

Step three: Rely on God's voice

In verse 10 Paul criticises those who rely on the Law, reminding them that their freedom lies in the promise of the Holy Spirit (v14). The Law was the path to life, and so it became the main focus of people's lives.

Now, the cross has done away with the Law and the Holy Spirit is our path to life. In the same way, the Spirit must be the focus of our lives, as we pursue more of God within us, working around us and inviting us onward.

Ultimately, we receive the Spirit by placing nothing else at the centre of our lives, so that he can live there. If we make space, he will come.

STUDY QUESTIONS

In what ways do you live "in your own strength" or do you push God to the edges?

Notes:

Have you found a sense of God's presence and/or Holy Spirit has made a difference in the past? If so, how?

Notes:

What are the voices that influence your life?

E.g. selfishness, pride, fashion, peer-pressure, society, media etc.

When have you heard God's voice in the past, or recently? Do you have any sense of him saying anything now?

Notes:

What might living by faith look like for you? What are the struggles that make this difficult?

Notes:

What do you put in the centre of your life? Have you invited the Holy Spirit to fill you today?

Notes:

Study Six

FREE TO LIVE FOR GOD

Galatians 3:15-25 and 6:1-18

A man reaps what he sows ... the one who sows to please the Spirit, from the Spirit will reap eternal life. Let us not become weary in doing good, for at the proper time we will receive a harvest.

Galatians 6:7-9

COMMENTARY

As we have worked our way through Galatians from the perspective of freedom, we might have noticed that another word Paul returns to is "promise." In our last study we read how in Galatians 3:1-14, Paul unpacked a brief theology of faith by looking at the life of Abraham. As we move on to 3:15-25, we find that he continues this line of thought, as he makes his way towards the heart of the matter.

We are free because of the promise that God made to Abraham, that "all peoples on earth will be blessed through you" (Genesis 12:3, and directly referred to by Paul in verse 8).

It was this promise that eventually led God to send his son Jesus, to show us the way of life before defeating death on the cross; and, as we discovered in our last study, it was this promise that led God to make a new promise to all who believed in Jesus: that He would not only live alongside them, but inside them by the Holy Spirit, working through them and extending his kingdom.

Having established their freedom to hear the gospel and their calling, their freedom from their former self and from the Law, Paul turns his attention to what should be the fruit of all this freedom: the freedom to live for God. And as he addresses this, he has two priorities to establish. The first, which he addresses in 3:15-25, is to do with the relationship that should result. The second, which he addresses in 6:1-18, is to do with the pursuit of a good life.

For Paul, the Law was a necessary stopgap between Abraham and Jesus. Abraham's faith was defined by his relationship with God and expressed by his willingness to walk with God. We can read through Abraham's life and identify plenty of moments when he seemed to be less than perfect - indeed, when he seemed to think and behave much as we all do - but his was not a life of rules.

What mattered to God was relationship and willingness, both of which Abraham had in spades! However, God's people fell into slavery and out of relationship with Him and so the Law was established to draw them back and show them what God's holiness really looked like.

Naturally, no-one could live up to God's standard, until Jesus. He displayed complete holiness, borne out of relationship with the Father and empowered by relationship with the Holy Spirit. Jesus lived for God and, in satisfying the Law on the cross, he restored our invitation to do the same. Our freedom, says Paul, compels us into a meaningful relationship with God.

Paul goes on to revisit each of the freedoms he has identified from the perspective of this relationship, as we have discovered in each of our studies, before finally coming back to issue of how we work this relationship out in real life: walking in freedom.

In chapter six, Paul concludes his letter with a series of practical encouragements: be gentle with those who struggle, but remain intent on a holy life, support one another, be humble, bless those who bless you, don't invest in things that harm you, invest in pleasing the Holy Spirit, live for doing good and do good for everyone, don't worry about outward appearances, live for God.

This is what a relationship with God in the power of the Holy Spirit looks like: practical decisions to love God and love others, to spend time with God and time with others, to bless God and bless others. Live for God in this way, says Paul, and you become a new creation.

APPLICATION

We continue to walk with all the same freedom as Paul describes in Galatians. We are free to know the gospel, free from our former self, free to hear God's calling, free to live by faith, free to live by the Spirit and free to live for God.

As such we should hear the urgency in Paul's voice just the same as the Galatians would have: God invites us into a life of relationship, not of rules, and only when we embrace this amazing, freeing revelation will we be walking in the freedom Jesus has won for us. This is no mystical truth. There is nothing of the mystery of faith here. Paul describes a relationship with God that is both very practical and dependent on others.

Salvation is not earned, and faith is not about how good we are at "following the rules," but the outworking of faith is to be found in our attitudes and our behaviour and it is sometimes tricky to see the dividing line. Faith based on rules is religion, not relationship, and although religion may help many of us draw us into God's presence, it is only the road and not the destination.

When it becomes the destination it in fact becomes a distraction from God, as we "perform" our faith, measuring ourselves against what is required of us rather than running the race, as Paul describes it, in which you look only at the finishing line, not at your own feet.

A relationship is only as good as the time you spend with the one you relate to. If we want our relationship with God to shape our lifestyle rather than rules shaping our relationship, then we need to spend time with God, talking to Him about what's going on in our life, and the lives of those around us, listening for him to talk to us about what he's doing and what matters to him, telling him he's great, letting him tell us the same, going out of our way to please him and stand up for him, and letting him do the same.

We do this through prayer, through reading the Bible (a guaranteed way of hearing his words to us!) and through living as we know he wants us to live. It's about two way communication and action, just the same as any other relationship, except that life with God goes so much further, because he sees so much more of us, does so much more in and through us and stays with us so much longer.

Paul's list of "good deeds" is extremely practical and shows us how we can invest in our relationship, and how we can live more for God, but it's amazing how many of these are to do with how we treat other people. Paul doesn't describe a relationship with God in isolation from those around us. Faith is best expressed when supporting, encouraging, blessing and being blessed by others.

Indeed, a healthy relationship with God relies on a community of believers living in faith together, bringing corporate worship, community support, mutual discipleship and kingdom co-operation (such as mission and evangelism, social justice, etc).

If we want our relationship with God to grow, then we need to spend time alone with God and time with the church. We need a community of faith around us, to help us become mature (as Paul says in Ephesians 4:13) and to step into the full calling that God has for us: to live with him and extend his kingdom.

This is the life that Jesus lived.

This is living by faith.

This is what walking in freedom is all about.

STUDY QUESTIONS

Is your faith expressed by "obeying the rules" or pursuing a relationship? How do you feel about that?

Notes:

How might you invest more in your relationship with God?

Notes:

Are there areas of your life where God is calling you to show more willingness to follow him?

Notes:

How are you loving God and loving others?

Notes:

Are you spending enough time with God and enough time with others?

Notes:

Do you make blessing God and blessing others a priority?

Notes:

Fountain Network

The Well Christian Centre
Swaffham Road
Ashill
Norfolk
IP25 7BT

www.fountainnetwork.org

Lightning Source UK Ltd.
Milton Keynes UK
UKOW040602191112

202406UK00001B/6/P